THE KAMA SUTRA

THE CLASSIC GUIDE TO LOVE

amber
BOOKS

First published in 2013 by
Amber Books Ltd
74–77 White Lion Street
London N1 9PF
Website: www.amberbooks.co.uk
Appstore: itunes.com/apps/amberbooksltd
Facebook: www.facebook.com/amberbooks
Twitter: @amberbooks

Reprinted in 2018

ISBN: 978-1-909160-22-4

Text: Adapted from original text by Vātsyāyana, translated by Richard Burton
Introduction: Edwin Collings-Wells
Project Editor: Sarah Uttridge
Design: Zöe Mellors

Printed and bound in Hong Kong

TRADITIONAL CHINESE BOOKBINDING
This book has been produced using traditional Chinese bookbinding
techniques, using a method that was developed during the Ming Dynasty
(1368–1644) and remained in use until the adoption of Western binding
techniques in the early 1900s. In traditional Chinese binding, single sheets of
paper are printed on one side only, and each sheet is folded in half, with the
printed pages on the outside. The book block is then sandwiched between
two boards and sewn together through punched holes close to the cut edges
of the folded sheets.

Contents

Introduction

The remarkable longevity of this well-known ancient Indian Hindu text is owed to the strength of its focus on personal betterment: virtue, enlightenment and hedonistic pursuits which have long concerned the human race.

The *Kama Sutra* is thought to have been composed some time between 400 BCE and 200 CE, though possibly not compiled into its present form until the 2nd century CE. Written by the Vedic Hindu philosopher Vatsyayana, it is regarded as one of the most authoritative scripts on human sexual behaviour. Vatsyayana composed the text in Sanskrit, an ancient Indo-Aryan language, and thus the *Kama Sutra* shares close links with Hinduism: *kama*, meaning sensual or sexual pleasure, represents one of the goals of Hindu life, while *sutra* refers to a manual made from a set of rules or formulas. Sanskrit is the chief holy language of Hinduism, and the word "Sanskrit" itself can be translated as a term for refined or elaborate speech.

Although commonly misperceived (especially in the Western world) as a sex manual, the text is, more accurately, a guide to leading a virtuous life and so focuses on holistic spirituality, rather than tantric sexual rites. The complete *Kama Sutra* includes seven sections written in prose and episodic anustubh verse, in which Vatsyayana pontificates on love, family and the more general aspects of a gracious, pleasurable life. This particular version is comprised of the chapters on sexual union and on attracting others to oneself.

This edition's translation originates from 1883 and is the most widely known English version. The translation is attributed to Sir Richard Francis Burton; however, several other people were involved in the undertaking too, including Indian archaeologist Bhagwanlal Indraji and Indian civil servant Forster Fitzgerald Arbuthnot. Burton acted as the publisher of his translation, and he added the footnotes that appear in this edition.

The striking illustrations that appear in this edition were made in the 17th and 18th centuries and were photographed by Roland and Sabrina Michaud during numerous trips to India over the last 40 years. Known as Oriental miniatures, the drawings were most likely created using a Persian tradition involving the use of vermilion. The colours, made from ground powder pigments, are bright and rich, mirroring Vatsyayana's vivid passages on sexual union. The absence of complete realism is typical of miniature illustrations; in the case of these images, the flailing, seemingly boneless limbs and the lack of any fully formed third dimension attest this. Artists preferred to avoid devoting time to worldly appearance, instead choosing to concentrate on the inherent spirituality of life, hence the abstractions.

The *Kama Sutra* is both acclaimed and infamous for its section on sex, and consequently has a reputation that reaches wider than its readers. However, it is those who take the time to enjoy its literary and, at times, very moving prose that know of its power as a spiritual companion. The fact that the *Kama Sutra* – so far removed from its original language, distributed widely across the world – is still held in such high and sacred regard says a great deal about its potential for personal enrichment.

CHAPTER 1
Kinds of sexual union

Man is divided into three classes, *viz.*, the hare man, the bull man, and the horse man, according to the size of his *lingam*.

Woman also, according to the depth of her *yoni*, is either a female deer, a mare, or a female elephant.

There are thus three equal unions between persons of corresponding dimensions, and there are six unequal unions, when the dimensions do not correspond, or nine in all, as the following table shows:

EQUAL		UNEQUAL	
MEN	WOMEN	MEN	WOMEN
Hare	Deer	Hare	Mare
Bull	Mare	Hare	Elephant
Horse	Elephant	Bull	Deer
		Bull	Elephant
		Horse	Deer
		Horse	Mare

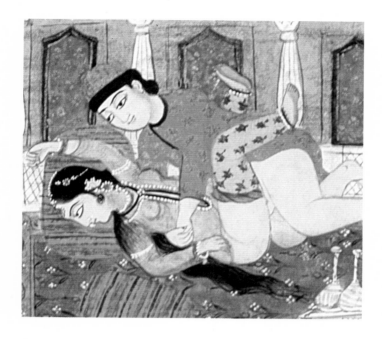

In these unequal unions, when the male exceeds the female in point of size, his union with a woman who is immediately next to him in size is called high union, and is of two kinds; while his union with the woman most remote from him in size is called the highest union, and is of one kind only. On the other hand when the female exceeds the male in point of size, her union with a man immediately next to her in size is called low union, and is of two kinds; while her union with a man most remote from her in size is called the lowest union, and is of one kind only.

In other words, the horse and mare, the bull and deer, form the high union, while the horse and deer form the highest union. On the female side, the elephant and bull, the mare and hare, form low unions, while the elephant and the hare make the lowest unions.

There are then, nine kinds of union according to dimensions. Amongst all these, equal unions are the best, those of a superlative degree, i.e. the highest and the lowest, are the worst, and the rest are middling, and with them the high[1] are better than the low.

1: High unions are said to be better than low ones, for in the former it is possible for the male to satisfy his own passion without injuring the female, while in the latter it is difficult for the female to be satisfied by any means.

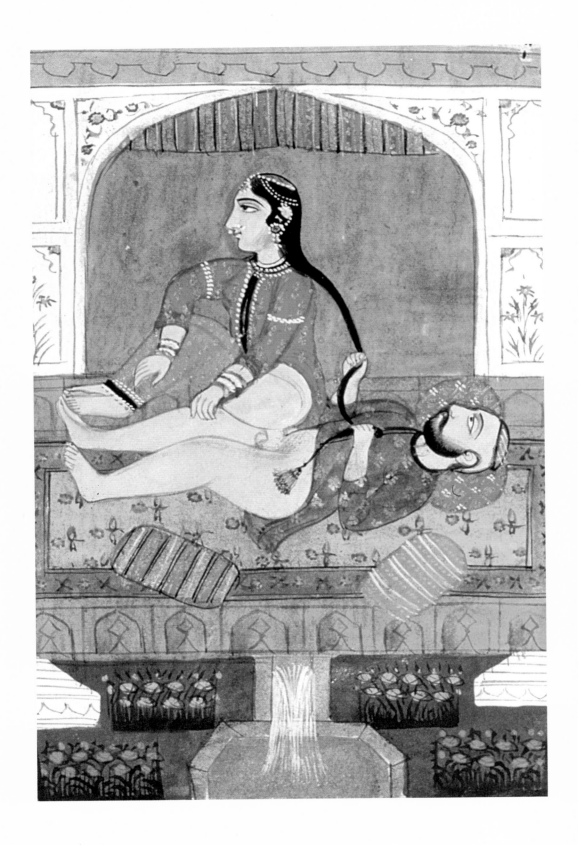

There are also nine kinds of union according to the force of passion or carnal desire, as follows:

MEN	WOMEN	MEN	WOMEN
Small	Small	Small	Middling
Middling	Middling	Small	Intense
Intense	Intense	Middling	Small
		Middling	Intense
		Intense	Small
		Intense	Middling

A man is called a man of small passion whose desire at the time of sexual union is not great, whose semen is scanty, and who cannot bear the warm embraces of the female.

Those who differ from this temperament are called men of middling passion, while those of intense passion are full of desire.

In the same way, women are supposed to have the three degrees of feeling as specified above.

Lastly, according to time there are three kinds of men and women, *viz.* the short-timed, the moderate-timed, and the long-timed, and of these as in the previous statements, there are nine kinds of union.

But on this last head there is a difference of opinion about the female, which should be stated.

Auddalika says, "Females do not emit as males do. The males simply remove their desire, while the females, from their consciousness of desire, feel a certain kind of pleasure, which gives them satisfaction, but it is impossible for them to tell you what kind of pleasure they feel. The fact from which this becomes evident is, that males, when engaged in coition, cease of themselves after emission, and are satisfied, but it is not so with females."

This opinion is, however, objected to on the grounds that if a male be long-timed, the female loves him the more, but if he be short-timed, she is dissatisfied with him. And this circumstance, some say, would prove that the female emits also.

But this opinion does not hold good, for if it takes a long time to allay a woman's desire, and during this time she is enjoying great pleasure, it is quite natural then that she should wish for its continuation. And on this subject there is a verse as follows:

"By union with men the lust, desire, or passion of women is satisfied, and the pleasure derived from the consciousness of it is called their satisfaction."

The followers of Babhravya, however, say that the semen of women continues to fall from the beginning of the sexual union to its end, and it is right that it should be so, for if they had no semen there would be no embryo.

To this there is an objection. In the beginning of coition the passion of the woman is middling, and she cannot bear the vigorous thrusts of her lover, but by degrees her passion increases until she ceases to think about her body, and then finally she wishes to stop from further coition.

This objection, however, does not hold good, for even in ordinary things that revolve with great force, such as a potter's wheel, or a top, we find that the motion at first is slow, but by degrees it becomes very rapid. In the same way the passion of the woman having gradually increased, she has a desire to discontinue coition, when all the semen has fallen away. And there is a verse with regard to this as follows:

"The fall of the semen of the man takes place only at the end of coition, while the semen of the woman falls continually, and after the semen of both has all fallen away then they wish for the discontinuance of coition."[2]

2: The strength of passion with women varies a great deal, some being easily satisfied, and others eager and willing to go on for a long time. To satisfy these last thoroughly a man must have recourse to art. It is certain that a fluid flows from the woman in larger or smaller quantities, but her satisfaction is not complete until she has experienced the "spasme génêsique", as described in a French work recently published and called "Breviare de l'Amour Experimental par le Dr. Jules Guyot".

Lastly, Vatsyayana is of the opinion that the semen of the female falls in the same way as that of the male.

Now some may ask here: If men and women are beings of the same kind, and are engaged in bringing about the same result, why should they have different works to do.

Vatsya says that this is so, because the ways of working as well as the consciousness of pleasure in men and women are different. The

difference in the ways of working, by which men are the actors, and women are the persons acted upon, is owing to the nature of the male and the female, otherwise the actor would be sometimes the person acted upon, and vice versa. And from this difference in the ways of working follows the difference in the consciousness of pleasure, for a man thinks, "this woman is united with me", and a woman thinks, "I am united with this man".

It may be said that if the ways of working in men and women are different, why should not there be a difference, even in the pleasure they feel, and which is the result of those ways.

But this objection is groundless, for the person acting and the person acted upon being of different kinds, there is a reason for the difference in their ways of working; but there is no reason for any difference in the pleasure they feel, because they both naturally derive pleasure from the act they perform.[3]

On this again some may say that when different persons are engaged in doing the same work, we find that they accomplish the same end or purpose: while, on the contrary, in the case of men and women we find that each of them accomplishes his or her own end separately, and this is inconsistent. But this is a mistake, for we find that sometimes two things are done at the same time, as for instance in the fighting of rams, both the rams receive the shock at the same time on their heads. Again, in throwing one wood apple against another, and also in a fight or struggle of wrestlers. If it be said that in these cases the things employed are of the same kind, it is answered that even in the case of men and women, the nature of the two persons is the same. And as the difference in their ways of working arises from the difference of their conformation only, it follows that men experience the same kind of pleasure as women do.

3: This is a long dissertation very common among Sanskrit authors, both when writing and talking socially. They start certain propositions, and then argue for and against them. What it is presumed the author means, is, that though both men and women derive pleasure from the act of coition, the way it is produced is brought about by different means, each individual performing his own work in the matter, irrespective of the other, and each deriving individually their own consciousness of pleasure from the act they perform. There is a difference in the work that each does, and a difference in the consciousness of pleasure that each has, but no difference in the pleasure they feel, for each feels that pleasure to a greater or lesser degree.

There is also a verse on this subject as follows: "Men and women being of the same nature, feel the same kind of pleasure, and therefore a man should marry such a woman as will love him ever afterwards."

The pleasure of men and women being thus proved to be of the same kind, it follows that in regard to time, there are nine kinds of sexual intercourse, in the same way as there are nine kinds, according to the force of passion.

There being thus nine kinds of union with regard to dimensions, force of passion, and time, respectively, by making combinations of them, innumerable kinds of union would be produced. Therefore in each particular kind of sexual union, men should use such means as they may think suitable for the occasion.[4]

At the first time of sexual union the passion of the male is intense, and his time is short, but in subsequent unions on the same day the reverse of this is the case. With the female, however, it is the contrary, for at the first time her passion is weak, and then her time long, but on subsequent occasions on the same day, her passion is intense and her time short, until her passion is satisfied.

On the different kinds of Love
Men learned in the humanities are of opinion that love is of four kinds

1. *Love acquired by continual habit*
Love resulting from the constant and continual performance and habit, as for instance the love of sexual intercourse, the love of hunting, the love of drinking, the love of gambling, etc., etc.

2. *Love resulting from the imagination*
Love which is felt for things to which we are not habituated, and which proceeds entirely from ideas, is called love resulting from imagination, as for instance, that love which some men and women and eunuchs feel for

---

4: This paragraph should be particularly noted, for it specially applies to married men and their wives. So many men utterly ignore the feelings of women, and never pay the slightest attention to the passion of the latter. To understand the subject thoroughly, it is absolutely necessary to study it, and then a person will know that, as dough is prepared for baking, so must a woman be prepared for sexual intercourse, if she is to derive satisfaction from it.

the Auparishtaka or mouth congress, and that which is felt by all for such things as embracing, kissing, etc., etc.

3. *Love resulting from belief*

The love which is mutual on both sides, and proved to be true, when each looks upon the other as his or her very own, such is called love resulting from belief by the learned.

4. *Love resulting from the perception of external objects*

The love resulting from the perception of external objects is quite evident and well-known to the world, because the pleasure which it affords is superior to the pleasure of the other kinds of love, which exists only for its sake.

What has been said in this chapter upon the subject of sexual union is sufficient for the learned; but for the edification of the ignorant, the same will now be treated of at length and in detail.

CHAPTER 2
Of the embrace

This part of the Kama Shastra, which treats of sexual union, is also called "Sixty-four" (*Chatushshashti*). Some old authors say that it is called so, because it contains sixty-four chapters. Others are of opinion that the author of this part being a person named Panchala, and the person who recited the part of the *Rig Veda* called *Dashatapa*, which contains sixty-four verses, being also called Panchala, the name "sixty-four" has been given to the part of the work in honour of the *Rig Vedas*. The followers of Babhravya say on the other hand that this part contains eight subjects, *viz.* the embrace, kissing, scratching with the nails or fingers, biting, lying down, making various sounds, playing the part of a man, and the *Auparishtaka*, or mouth congress. Each of these subjects being of eight kinds, and eight multiplied by eight being sixty-four, this part is therefore named "sixty-four". But Vatsyayana affirms that as this part contains also the following subjects, *viz.* striking, crying, the acts of a man during congress, the various kinds of congress, and other subjects, the name "sixty-four" is given to it only accidentally. As, for instance, we say this tree is "*Saptaparna*", or seven-leaved, this offering of rice is "*Panchavarna*", or five-coloured, but the tree has not seven leaves, neither has the rice five colours.

However, the part sixty-four is now treated of, and the embrace, being the first subject, will now be considered.

Now the embrace which indicates the mutual love of a man and woman who have come together is of four kinds:

The action in each case is denoted by the meaning of the word which stands for it.

1. *Touching*
When a man under some pretext or other goes in front or alongside of a woman and touches her body with his own, it is called the "touching embrace".

2. *Piercing*

When a woman in a lonely place bends down, as if to pick up something, and pierces, as it were, a man sitting or standing, with her breasts, and the man in return takes hold of them, it is called a "piercing embrace".

> The above two kinds of embrace take place only between persons who do not, as yet, speak freely with each other.

3. *Rubbing*

When two lovers are walking slowly together, either in the dark, or in a place of public resort, or in a lonely place, and rub their bodies against each other, it is called a "rubbing embrace".

4. *Pressing*

When on the above occasion one of them presses the other's body forcibly against a wall or pillar, it is called a "pressing embrace".

> These two last embraces are peculiar to those who know the intentions of each other.

At the time of the meeting the four following kinds of embrace are used:

1. *Jataveshtitaka*, or the twining of a creeper

When a woman, clinging to a man as a creeper twines round a tree, bends his head down to hers with the desire of kissing him and slightly makes the sound of *sut sut*, embraces him, and looks lovingly towards him, it is called an embrace like the "twining of a creeper".

2. *Vrikshadhirudhaka*, or climbing a tree

When a woman, having placed one of her feet on the foot of her lover, and the other on one of his thighs, passes one of her arms round his back, and the other on his shoulders, makes slightly the sounds of singing and cooing, and wishes, as it were, to climb up him in order to have a kiss, it is called an embrace like the "climbing of a tree".

> These two kinds of embrace take place when the lover is standing.

3. *Tila-Tandulaka,* or the mixture of sesamum seed with rice
When lovers lie on a bed, and embrace each other so closely that the
arms and thighs of the one are encircled by the arms and thighs of the
other, and are, as it were, rubbing up against them, this is called an
embrace like "the mixture of sesamum seed with rice".

4. *Kshiraniraka*, or milk and water embrace
When a man and a woman are very much in love with each other, and
not thinking of any pain or hurt, embrace each other as if they were
entering into each other's bodies, either while the woman is sitting on
the lap of the man or in front of him, or on a bed, then it is called an
embrace like a "mixture of milk and water".

These two kinds of embrace take place at the time of sexual union.
Babhravya has thus related to us the above eight kinds of embraces.

Suvarnanabha, moreover, gives us four ways of embracing simple members of the body, which are:

1. *The embrace of the thighs*
When one of two lovers presses forcibly one or both of the thighs of the other between his or her own, it is called the "embrace of thighs".

2. *The embrace of the jaghana, i.e. the part of the body from the navel downwards to the thighs.*
When a man presses the *jaghana* or middle part of the woman's body against his own, and mounts upon her to practise, either scratching with the nail or finger, or biting, or striking, or kissing, the hair of the woman being loose and flowing, it is called the "embrace of the *jaghana*".

3. *The embrace of the breasts*
When a man places his breast between the breasts of a woman, and presses her with it, it is called the "embrace of the breasts".

4. *The embrace of the forehead*
When either of the lovers touches the mouth, the eyes and the forehead of the other with his or her own, it is called the "embrace of the forehead".

Some say that even shampooing is a kind of embrace, because there is a touching of bodies in it. But Vatsyayana thinks that shampooing is performed at a different time, and for a different purpose, and it is also of a different character, it cannot be said to be included in the embrace.

There are also some verses on the subject as follows:

> *"The whole subject of embracing is of such a nature that men who ask questions about it, or who hear about it, or who talk about it, acquire thereby a desire for enjoyment. Even those embraces that are not mentioned in the Kama Shastra should be practised at the time of sexual enjoyment, if they are in any way conducive to the increase of love or passion. The rules of the Shastra apply so long as the passion of man is middling, but when the wheel of love is once set in motion, there is then no Shastra and no order."*

CHAPTER 3

On kissing

It is said by some that there is no fixed time or order between the
embrace, the kiss, and the pressing or scratching with the nails or
fingers, but that all these things should be done generally before
sexual union takes place, while striking and making the various sounds
generally takes place at the time of the union. Vatsyayana, however,
thinks that anything may take place at any time, for love does not care
for time or order.

On the occasion of the first congress, kissing and the other things
mentioned above should be done moderately, they should not be
continued for a long time, and should be done alternately. On
subsequent occasions, however, the reverse of all this may take place, and
moderation will not be necessary, they may continue for a long time, and
for the purpose of kindling love, they may be all done at the same time.

The following are the places for kissing, *viz.* the forehead, the eyes,
the cheeks, the throat, the bosom, the breasts, the lips, and the interior
of the mouth. Moreover, the people of the Lat country kiss also on the
following places, *viz.* the joints of the thighs, the arms, and the navel. But
Vatsyayana thinks that though kissing is practised by these people in the
above places on account of the intensity of their love, and the customs of
their country, it is not fit to be practised by all.

Now in a case of a young girl there are three sort of kisses:

1. *The nominal kiss*
When a girl only touches the mouth of her lover with her own, but does not herself do anything, it is called the "nominal kiss".

2. *The throbbing kiss*

When a girl, setting aside her bashfulness a little, wishes to touch the lip that is pressed into her mouth, and with that object moves her lower lip, but not the upper one, it is called the "throbbing kiss".

3. *The touching kiss*

When a girl touches her lover's lip with her tongue, and having shut her eyes, places her hands on those of her lover, it is called the "touching kiss".

Other authors describe four other kinds of kisses, *viz.*:

1. *The straight kiss*

When the lips of two lovers are brought into direct contact with each other, it is called a "straight kiss".

2. *The bent kiss*

When the heads of two lovers are bent towards each other, and when so bent kissing takes place, it is called a "bent kiss".

3. *The turned kiss*

When one of them turns up the face of the other by holding the head and chin, and then kissing, it is called a "turned kiss".

4. *The pressed kiss*

Lastly, when the lower lip is pressed with much force, it is called a "pressed kiss".

There is also a fifth kind of kiss called the "greatly pressed kiss", which is effected by taking hold of the lower lip between two fingers, and then after touching it with the tongue, pressing it with great force with the lip.

As regards kissing, a wager may be laid as to which will get hold of the lips of the other first. If the woman loses, she should pretend to cry, should keep her lover off by shaking her hands, and turn away from him and dispute with him, saying "let another wager be laid". If she

loses this a second time, she should appear doubly distressed, and when her lover is off his guard or asleep, she should get hold of his lower lip, and hold it in her teeth, so that it should not slip away, and then she should laugh, make a loud noise, deride him, dance about, and say whatever she likes in a joking way, moving her eyebrows, and rolling her eyes. Such are the wagers and quarrels as far as kissing is concerned, but the same may be applied with regard to the pressing or scratching with the nails and fingers, biting and striking. All these, however, are only peculiar to men and women of intense passion.

When a man kisses the upper lip of a woman, while she in return kisses his lower lip, it is called the "kiss of the upper lip".

When one of them takes both the lips of the other between his or her own, it is called "a clasping kiss". A woman, however, only takes this kind of kiss from a man who has no moustache. And on the occasion of this kiss, if one of them touches the teeth, the tongue, and the palate of the other, with his or her tongue, it is called the "fighting of the tongue". In the same way, the pressing of the teeth of the one against the mouth of the other is to be practised.

Kissing is of four kinds, *viz.* moderate, contracted, pressed, and soft, according to the different parts of the body which are kissed, for different kinds of kisses are appropriate for different parts of the body.

When a woman looks at the face of her lover while he is asleep, and kisses it to show her intention or desire, it is called a "kiss that kindles love".

When a woman kisses her lover while he is engaged in business, or while he is quarrelling with her, or while he is looking at something else, so that his mind may be turned away, it is called a "kiss that turns away".

When a lover coming home late at night kisses his beloved, who is asleep or in bed, in order to show her his desire, it is called a "kiss that awakens". On such an occasion the woman may pretend to be asleep at the time of her lover's arrival, so that she may know his intention and obtain respect from him.

When a person kisses the reflection of the person he loves in a mirror, in water, or on a wall, it is called a "kiss showing the intention".

When a person kisses a child sitting on his lap, or a picture, or an image, or figure, in the presence of the person beloved by him, it is called a "transferred kiss".

When at night at a theatre, or in an assembly of caste men, a man coming up to a woman kisses a finger of her hand if she be standing, or a toe of her foot if she be sitting, or when a woman is shampooing her lover's body, places her face on his thigh (as if she was sleepy) so as to inflame his passion, and kisses his thigh or great toe, it is called a "demonstrative kiss".

There is also a verse on the subject as follows:

"Whatever things may be done by one of the lovers to the other,
the same should be returned by the other, i.e. if the woman kisses him
he should kiss her in return, if she strikes him he should also
strike her in return."

CHAPTER 4

On pressing, or marking, or scratching with the nails

When love becomes intense, pressing with the nails or scratching the body with them is practised, and it is done on the following occasions: On the first visit; at the time of setting out on a journey; on the return from a journey; at the time when an angry lover is reconciled; and lastly when the woman is intoxicated.

But pressing with the nails is not a usual thing except with those who are intensely passionate, i.e. full of passion. It is employed together with biting, by those to whom the practice is agreeable.

Pressing with the nails is of the eight following kinds, according to the forms of the marks which are produced:

1. *Sounding*
When a person presses the chin, the breasts, the lower lip, or the *jaghana* of another so softly that no scratch or mark is left, but only the hair on the body becomes erect from the touch of the nails, and the nails themselves make a sound, it is called a "sounding or pressing with the nails".

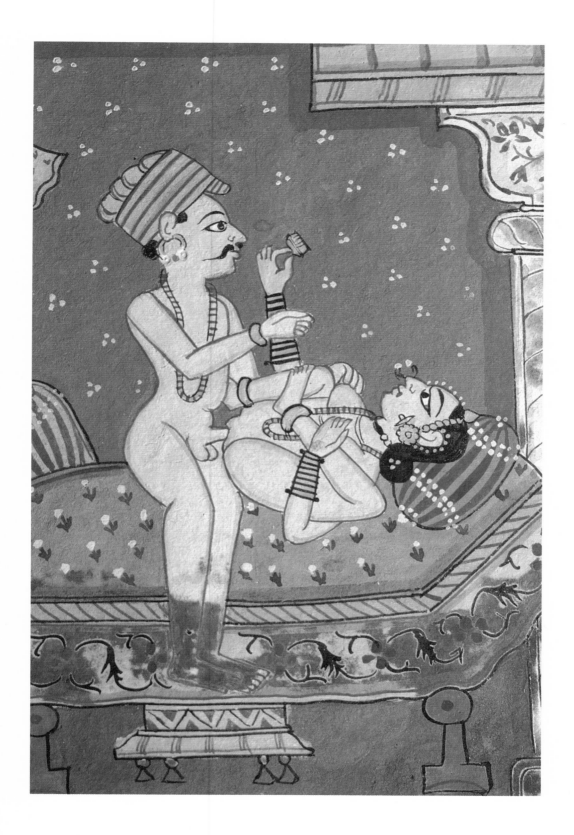

This pressing is used in the case of a young girl when her lover shampoos her, scratches her head, and wants to trouble or frighten her.

2. *Half moon*
The curved mark with the nails, which is impressed on the neck and the breasts, is called the "half moon".

3. *A circle*
When the half moons are impressed opposite to each other, it is called a "circle". This mark with the nails is generally made on the navel, the small cavities about the buttocks, and on the joints of the thigh.

4. *A line*
A mark in the form of a small line, and which can be made on any part of the body, is called a "line".

5. *A tiger's nail or claw*
This same line, when it is curved, and made on the breast, is called a "tiger's nail".

6. *A peacock's foot*
When a curved mark is made on the breast by means of the five nails, it is called a "peacock's foot". This mark is made with the object of being praised, for it requires a great deal of skill to make it properly.

7. *The jump of a hare*
When five marks with the nails are made close to one another near the nipple of the breast, it is called "the jump of a hare".

8. *The leaf of a blue lotus*
A mark made on the breast or on the hips in the form of a leaf of the blue lotus, is called the "leaf of a blue lotus".

The places that are to be pressed with the nails are as follows: the armpit, the throat, the breasts, the lips, the *jaghana*, or middle parts of the body, and the thighs. But Suvarnanabha is of opinion that when the impetuosity of passion is excessive, then the places need not be considered.

The qualities of good nails are that they should be bright, well set, clean, entire, convex, soft, and glossy in appearance. Nails are of three kinds according to their size:

1. *Small*
Small nails, which can be used in various ways, and are to be applied only with the object of giving pleasure, are possessed by the people of the southern districts.

2. *Middling*

Middling nails, which contain the properties of both the above kinds, belong to the people of the Maharashtra.

3. *Large*

Large nails, which give grace to the hands, and attract the hearts of women from their appearance, are possessed by the Bengalees.

When a person is going on a journey, and makes a mark on the thighs, or on the breast, it is called a "token of remembrance". On such an occasion three or four lines are impressed close to one another with the nails.

Here ends the marking with the nails. Marks of other kinds than the above may also be made with the nails, for the ancient authors say, that as there are innumerable degrees of skill among men (the practice of this art being known to all), so there are innumerable ways of making these marks. And as pressing or marking with the nails is independent of love, no one can say with certainty how many different kinds of marks with the nails do actually exist. The reason of this is, Vatsyayana says, that as variety is necessary in love, so love is to be produced by means of variety. It is on this account that courtesans, who are well acquainted with various ways and means, become so desirable, for if variety is sought in all the arts and amusements, such as archery and others, how much more should it be sought after in the present case.

The marks of the nails should not be made on married women, but particular kinds of marks may be made on their private parts for the remembrance and increase of love.

There are also some verses on the subject, as follows:

"The love of a woman who sees the marks of nails on the private parts of her body, even though they are old and almost worn out, becomes again fresh and new. If there be no marks of nails to remind a person of the passages of love, then love is lessened in the same way as when no union takes place for a long time."

Even when a stranger sees at a distance a young woman with the marks of nails on her breast,[5] he is filled with love and respect for her.

A man, also, who carries the marks of nails and teeth on some parts of his body, influences the mind of a woman, even though it be ever so firm. In short, nothing tends to increase love so much as the effects of marking with the nails, and biting.

5: From this it would appear that in ancient times the breasts of women were not covered, and this is seen in the painting of the *Ajunta* and other caves, where we find that the breasts of even royal ladies and others are exposed.

CHAPTER 5

On biting, and the means to be employed with regard to women of different countries

All the places that can be kissed, are also the places that can be bitten, except the upper lip, the interior of the mouth, and the eyes.

The qualities of good teeth are as follows: They should be equal, possessed of a pleasing brightness, capable of being coloured, of proper proportions, unbroken, and with sharp ends.

The defects of teeth on the other hand are, that they are blunt, protruding from the gums, rough, soft, large, and loosely set.

The following are the different kinds of biting:

1. *The hidden bite*
The biting which is shown only by the excessive redness of the skin that is bitten, is called the "hidden bite".

2. *The swollen bite*
When the skin is pressed down on both sides, it is called the "swollen bite".

3. *The point*
When a small portion of the skin is bitten with two teeth only, it is called the "point".

4. *The line of points*
When such small portions of the skin are bitten with all the teeth, it is called the "line of points".

5. *The coral and the jewel*

The biting which is done by bringing together the teeth and the lips, is called the "coral and the jewel". The lip is the coral, and the teeth the jewel.

6. *The line of jewels*

When biting is done with all the teeth, it is called the "line of jewels".

7. *The broken cloud*

The biting which consists of unequal risings in a circle, and which comes from the space between the teeth, is called the "broken cloud". This is impressed on the breasts.

8. *The biting of the boar*

The biting which consists of many broad rows of marks near to one another, and with red intervals, is called the "biting of a boar". This is impressed on the breasts and the shoulders; and these two last modes of biting are peculiar to persons of intense passion.

The lower lip is the place on which the "hidden bite", the "swollen bite", and the "point" are made; again the "swollen bite", and the "coral and the jewel" bite are done on the cheek. Kissing, pressing with the nails, and biting are the ornaments of the left cheek, and when the word cheek is used it is to be understood as the left cheek.

Both the "line of points" and the "line of jewels" are to be impressed on the throat, the armpit, and the joints of the thighs; but the "line of points" alone is to be impressed on the forehead and the thighs.

The marking with the nails, and the biting of the following things, *viz.* an ornament of the forehead, an ear ornament, a bunch of flowers, a betel leaf, or a *tamala* leaf, which are worn by, or belong to the woman that is beloved, are signs of the desire of enjoyment.

Here end the different kinds of biting.

*　　*　　*　　*　　*

In the affairs of love a man should do such things as are agreeable to the women of different countries.

The women of the central countries (i.e. between the Ganges and
the Jumna) are noble in their character, not accustomed to disgraceful
practices, and dislike pressing the nails and biting.

The women of the Balhika country are gained over by striking.

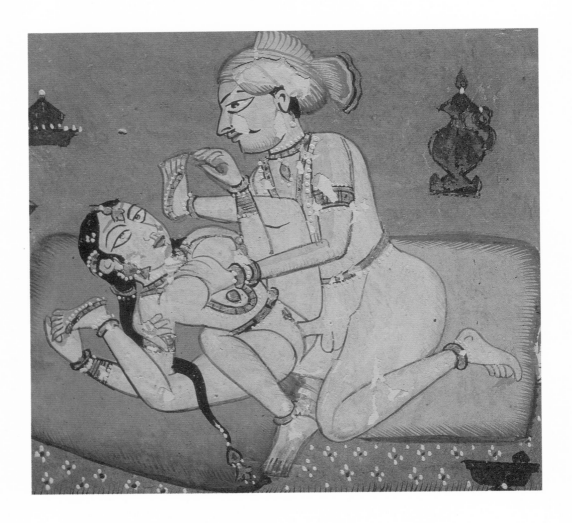

The women of Avantika are fond of foul pleasures, and have not good manners.

The women of the Maharashtra are fond of practising the sixty-four arts, they utter low and harsh words, and like to be spoken to in the same way, and have an impetuous desire of enjoyment.

The women of Pataliputra (i.e. the modern Patna) are of the same nature as the women of the Maharashtra, but show their likings only in secret.

The women of the Dravida country, though they are rubbed and pressed about at the time of sexual enjoyment, have a slow fall of semen, that is they are very slow in the act of coition.

The women of Vanavasi are moderately passionate, they go through every kind of enjoyment, cover their bodies, and abuse those who utter low, mean and harsh words.

The women of Avanti hate kissing, marking with the nails, and biting, but they have a fondness for various kinds of sexual union.

The women of Malwa like embracing and kissing, but not wounding, and they are gained over by striking.

The women of Abhira, and those of the country about the Indus and five rivers (i.e. the Punjab), are gained over by the *Auparishtaka* or mouth congress.

The women of Aparatika are full of passion, and make slowly the sound "Sit".

The women of the Lat country have even more impetuous desire, and also make the sound "Sit".

The women of the Stri Rajya, and of Koshola (Oude), are full of

impetuous desire, their semen falls in large quantities, and they are fond of taking medicine to make it do so.

The women of the Audhra country have tender bodies, they are fond of enjoyment, and have a liking for voluptuous pleasures.

The women of Ganda have tender bodies, and speak sweetly.

Now Suvarnanabha is of opinion that that which is agreeable to the nature of a particular person, is of more consequence than that which is agreeable to a whole nation, and that therefore the peculiarities of the country should not be observed in such cases. The various pleasures, the dress, and the sports of one country are in time borrowed by another, and in such a case these things must be considered as belonging originally to that country.

Among the things mentioned above, *viz.* embracing, kissing, etc. those which increase passion should be done first, and those which are only for amusement or variety should be done afterwards.

There are also some verses on this subject as follows:

"When a man bites a woman forcibly, she should angrily do the same
to him with double force. Thus a 'point' should be returned with a
'line of points', and a 'line of points' with a 'broken cloud', and if she be
excessively chafed, she should at once begin a love quarrel with him.
At such a time she should take hold of her lover by the hair,
and bend his head down, and kiss his lower lip, and then, being intoxicated
with love, she should shut her eyes and bite him in various places.
Even by day, and in a place of public resort, when her lover shows her
any mark that she may have inflicted on his body, she should
smile at the sight of it, and turning her face as if she were going
to chide him, she should show him with an angry look the marks on her
own body that have been made by him. Thus if men and women act
according to each other's liking, their love for each other will
not be lessened even in one hundred years."

CHAPTER 6

Of the different ways of lying down, and various kinds of congress

On the occasion of a "high congress" the *Mrigi* (deer) woman should lie down in such a way as to widen her *yoni*, while in a "low congress" the *Hastini* (elephant) woman should lie down so as to contract hers. But in an "equal congress" they should lie down in the natural position. What is said above concerning the *Mrigi* and the *Hastini* applies also to the *Vadawa* (mare) woman. In a "low congress" the woman should particularly make use of medicine, to cause her desires to be satisfied quickly.

The deer woman has the following three ways of lying down:

1. *The widely opened position*
When she lowers her head and raises her middle parts, it is called the "widely opened position". At such a time the man should apply some unguent, so as to make the entrance easy.

2. *The yawning position*

When she raises her thighs and keeps them wide apart and engages in congress, it is called the "yawning position".

3. *The position of the wife of Indra*

When she places her thighs with her legs doubled on them upon her sides, and thus engages in congress, it is called the position of Indrani,

and this is learnt only by practice. The position is also useful in the case of the "highest congress".

The "clasping position" is used in "low congress", and in the "lowest congress", together with the "pressing position", the "twining position", and the "mare's position".

When the legs of both the male and the female are stretched straight out over each other, it is called the "clasping position". It is of two kinds, the side position and the supine position, according to the way in which they lie down. In the side position the male should invariably lie on his left side, and cause the woman to lie on her right side, and this rule is to be observed in lying down with all kinds of women.

When, after congress has begun in the clasping position, the woman presses her lover with her thighs, it is called the "pressing position".

When the woman places one of her thighs across the thigh of her lover, it is called the "twining position".

When a woman forcibly holds in her *yoni* the *lingam* after it is in, it is called the "mare's position". This is learnt by practice only, and is chiefly found among the women of the Andra country.

The above are the different ways of lying down, mentioned by Babhravya; Suvarnanabha, however, gives the following in addition.

When the female raises both of her thighs straight up, it is called the "rising position".

When she raises both of her legs, and places them on her lover's shoulders, it is called the "yawning position".

When the legs are contracted, and thus held by the lover before his bosom, it is called the "pressed position".

When only one of her legs is stretched out, it is called the "half pressed position".

When the woman places one of her legs on her lover's shoulder, and stretches the other out, and then places the latter on his shoulder, and stretches out the other, and continues to do so alternately, it is called the "splitting of a bamboo".

When one of her legs is placed on the head, and the other is stretched out, it is called the "fixing of a nail". This is learnt by practice only.

When both the legs of the woman are contracted, and placed on her stomach, it is called the "crab's position".

When the thighs are raised and placed one upon the other, it is called the "packed position".

When the shanks are placed one upon the other, it is called the "lotus-like position".

When a man, during congress, turns round, and enjoys the woman without leaving her, while she embraces him round the back all the time, it is called the "turning position", and is learnt only by practice.

Thus says Suvarnanabha, these different ways of lying down, sitting, and standing should be practised in water, because it is easy to do so therein. But Vatsyayana is of opinion that congress in water is improper, because it is prohibited by the religious law.

When a man and a woman support themselves on each other's bodies, or on a wall, or pillar, and thus while standing engage in congress, it is called the "supported congress".

When a man supports himself against a wall, and the woman, sitting on his hands joined together and held underneath her, throws her arms round his neck, and putting her thighs alongside his waist, moves herself by her feet, which are touching the wall against which the man is leaning, it is called the "suspended congress".

When a woman stands on her hands and feet like a quadruped, and her lover mounts her like a bull, it is called the "congress of a cow". At this time everything that is ordinarily done on the bosom should be done on the back.

In the same way can be carried on the congress of a dog, the congress of a goat, the congress of a deer, the forcible mounting of an ass, the congress of a cat, the jump of a tiger, the pressing of an elephant, the rubbing of a boar, and the mounting of a horse. And in all these cases the characteristics of these different animals should be manifested by acting like them.

When a man enjoys two women at the same time, both of whom love him equally, it is called the "united congress".

When a man enjoys many women altogether, it is called the "congress of a herd of cows".

The following kinds of congress, *viz.* sporting in water, or the congress of an elephant with many female elephants, which is said to take place only in the water, the congress of a collection of goats, the congress of a collection of deer, take place in imitation of these animals.

In Gramaneri many young men enjoy a woman that may be married to one of them, either one after the other, or at the same time. Thus one of them holds her, another enjoys her, a third uses her mouth, a fourth holds her middle part, and in this way they go on enjoying her several parts alternately.

The same things can be done when several men are sitting in company with one courtesan, or when one courtesan is alone with many men. In the same way this can be done by the women of the King's harem when they accidentally get hold of a man.

The people in the Southern countries have also a congress in the anus, that is called the "lower congress".

Thus ends the various kinds of congress. There are also two verses on the subject as follows.

"An ingenious person should multiply the kinds of congress after the fashion of the different kinds of beasts and of birds. For these different kinds of congress, performed according to the usage of each country, and the liking of each individual, generate love, friendship, and respect in the hearts of women."

47

CHAPTER 7

Of the various modes of striking, and of the sounds appropriate to them

Sexual intercourse can be compared to a quarrel, on account of the contrarieties of love and its tendency to dispute. The place of striking with passion is the body, and on the body the special places are:

The shoulders.
The head.
The space between the breasts.
The back.
The *jaghana*, or middle part of the body.
The sides.

Striking is of four kinds, *viz.*

Striking with the back of the hand.
Striking with the fingers a little contracted.
Striking with the fist.
Striking with the open palm of the hand.

On account of its causing pain, striking gives rise to the hissing sound, which is of various kinds, and to the eight kinds of crying, *viz.*

The sound *Hin.*
The thundering sound.
The cooing sound.
The weeping sound.
The sound *Phut.*
The sound *Phât.*
The sound *Sût.*
The sound *Plât.*

Besides these, there are also words having a meaning, such as "mother", and those that are expressive of prohibition, sufficiency, desire of liberation, pain or praise, and to which may be added sounds like those of the dove, the cuckoo, the green pigeon, the parrot, the bee, the sparrow, the flamingo, the duck, and the quail, which are all occasionally made use of.

Blows with the fist should be given on the back of the woman, while she is sitting on the lap of the man, and she should give blows in return, abusing the man as if she were angry, and making the cooing and the weeping sounds. While the woman is engaged in congress the space between the breasts should be struck with the back of the hand, slowly at first, and then proportionately to the increasing excitement, until the end.

At this time the sounds *Hin* and others may be made, alternately or optionally, according to habit. When the man, making the sound *Phât*, strikes the woman on the head, with the fingers of his hand a little contracted, it is called *Prasritaka*, which means striking with the fingers of the hand a little contracted. In this case the appropriate sounds are the cooing sound, the sound *Phât*, and the sound *Phut* in the interior of the mouth, and at the end of congress the sighing and weeping sounds. The sound *Phât* is an imitation of the sound of a bamboo being split, while the sound *Phut* is like the sound made by something falling into water. At all times when kissing and such like things are begun, the woman should give a reply with a hissing sound. During the excitement when the woman is not accustomed to striking, she continually utters words expressive of prohibition, sufficiency, or desire of liberation, as well as the words "father", "mother", intermingled with the sighing, weeping and thundering sounds.[6] Towards the conclusion of the congress, the breasts, the *jaghana*, and the sides of the woman should be pressed with the open palms of the hand, with some force, until the end of it, and then sounds like those of the quail, or the goose should be made.

There are also two verses on the subject as follows:

6: Men who are well acquainted with the art of love are well aware how often one woman differs from another in her sighs and sounds during the time of congress. Some women like to be talked to in the most loving way, others in the most abusive way, and so on. Some women enjoy themselves with closed eyes in silence, others make a great noise over it, and some almost faint away. The great art is to ascertain what gives them the greatest pleasure, and what specialities they like best.

"The characteristics of manhood are said to consist of roughness
and impetuosity, while weakness, tenderness, sensibility, and an inclination
to turn away from unpleasant things are the distinguishing marks of
womanhood. The excitement of passion, and peculiarities of habit
may sometimes cause contrary results to appear, but these do not last long,
and in the end the natural state is resumed."

The wedge on the bosom, the scissors on the head, the piercing instrument on the cheeks, and the pinchers on the breasts and sides, may also be taken into consideration with the other four modes of striking, and thus give eight ways altogether. But these four ways of striking with instruments are peculiar to the people of the southern countries, and the marks caused by them are seen on the breasts of their women. They are local peculiarities, but Vatsyayana is of opinion that the practice of them is painful, barbarous, and base, and quite unworthy of imitation.

In the same way anything that is a local peculiarity should not always be adopted elsewhere, and even in the place where the practice is prevalent, excess of it should always be avoided. Instances of the dangerous use of them may be given as follows. The King of the Panchalas killed the courtesan Madhavasena by means of the wedge during congress. King Shatakarni Shatavahana of the Kuntalas deprived his great Queen Malayavati of her life by a pair of sssors, and Naradeva, whose hand was deformed, blinded a dancing girl by directing a piercing instrument in a wrong way.

There are also two verses on the subject as follows:

"About these things there cannot be either enumeration or any definite rule. Congress having once commenced, passion alone gives birth to all the acts of the parties."

Such passionate actions and amorous gesticulations or movements, which arise on the spur of the moment, and during sexual intercourse, cannot be defined, and are as irregular as dreams. A horse having once attained the fifth degree of motion goes on with blind speed, regardless of pits, ditches, and posts in his way; and in the same manner a loving pair become blind with passion in the heat of congress, and go on with great impetuosity, paying not the least regard to excess. For this reason one who is well acquainted with the science of love, and knowing his own strength, as also the tenderness, impetuosity, and strength of the young woman, should act accordingly. The various modes of enjoyment are not for all times or for all persons, but they should only be used at the proper time, and in the proper countries and places.

CHAPTER 8

About women acting the part of a man; and of the work of a man

When a woman sees that her lover is fatigued by constant congress, without having his desire satisfied, she should, with his permission, lay him down upon his back, and give him assistance by acting his part. She may also do this to satisfy the curiosity of her lover, or her own desire of novelty.

There are two ways of doing this: the first is when during congress she turns round, and gets on the top of her lover, in such a manner as to continue the congress, without obstructing the pleasure of it; and the other is when she acts the man's part from the beginning. At such a time, with flowers in her hair hanging loose, and her smiles broken by hard breathings, she should press upon her lover's bosom with her own breasts, and lowering her head frequently, should do in return the same actions which he used to do before, returning his blows and chaffing him, should say, "I was laid down by you, and fatigued with hard congress, I shall now therefore lay you down in return." She should then again manifest her own bashfulness, her fatigue, and her desire of stopping the congress. In this way she should do the work of a man, which we shall presently relate.

Whatever is done by a man for giving pleasure to a woman is called the work of a man, and is as follows:

While the woman is lying on his bed, and is as it were abstracted by his conversation, he should loosen the knot of her undergarments, and when she begins to dispute with him, he should overwhelm her with kisses. Then when his *lingam* is erect he should touch her with his hands in various places, and gently manipulate various parts of the body. If the woman is bashful, and if it is the first time that they have come together, the man should place his hands between her thighs, which she would probably keep close together, and if she is a very young girl, he should first get his hands upon her breasts, which she would probably cover with her own hands, and under her armpits and on her neck. If however she is a seasoned woman, he should do whatever is agreeable either to him or to her, and whatever is fitting for the occasion. After this he should

take hold of her hair, and hold her chin in his fingers for the purpose of kissing her. On this, if she is a young girl, she will become bashful and close her eyes. Any how he should gather from the action of the woman what things would be pleasing to her during congress.

Here Suvarnanabha says that while a man is doing to the woman what he likes best during congress, he should always make a point of pressing those parts of her body on which she turns her eyes.

The signs of the enjoyment and satisfaction of the women are as follows: her body relaxes, she closes her eyes, she puts aside all bashfulness, and shows increased willingness to unite the two organs as closely together as possible. On the other hand, the signs of her want of enjoyment and of failing to be satisfied are as follows: she shakes her hands, she does not let the man get up, feels dejected, bites the man, kicks him, and continues to go on moving after the man has finished. In such cases the man should rub the *yoni* of the woman with his hand and fingers (as the elephant rubs anything with his trunk) before engaging in congress, until it is softened, and after that is done he should proceed to put his *lingam* into her.

The acts to be done by the man are:

1. *Moving forward*
When the organs are brought together properly and directly it is called "moving the organ forward".

2. *Friction or churning*
When the *lingam* is held with the hand, and turned all round in the *yoni*, it is called "churning".

3. *Piercing*
When the *yoni* is lowered, and the upper part of it is struck with the *lingam*, it is called "piercing".

4. *Rubbing*
When the same thing is done on the lower part of the *yoni*, it is called "rubbing".

5. *Pressing*
When the *yoni* is pressed by the *lingam* for a long time, it is called "pressing".

6. *Giving a blow*
When the *lingam* is removed to some distance from the *yoni*, and then forcibly strikes it, it is called "giving a blow".

7. *The blow of a boar*
When only one part of the *yoni* is rubbed with the *lingam*, it is called the "blow of a boar".

8. *The blow of a bull*
When both sides of the *yoni* are rubbed in this way, it is called the "blow of a bull".

9. *The sporting of a sparrow*
When the *lingam* is in the *yoni*, and moved up and down frequently, and without being taken out, it is called the "sporting of a sparrow".

This takes place at the end of congress.

When a woman acts the part of a man, she has the following things to do in addition to the nine given above:

1. *The pair of tongs*
When the woman holds the *lingam* in her *yoni*, draws it in, presses it, and keeps it thus in her for a long time, it is called the "pair of tongs".

2. *The top*
When, while engaged in congress, she turns round like a wheel, it is called the "top". This is learnt by practice only.

3. *The swing*
When, on such an occasion, the man lifts up the middle part of his body, and the woman turns round her middle part, it is called the "swing".

When the woman is tired, she should place her forehead on that of her lover, and should thus take rest without disturbing the union of the organs, and when the woman has rested herself the man should turn round and begin the congress again.
  There are also some verses on the subject as follows:

"Though a woman is reserved, and keeps her feelings concealed,
yet when she gets on top of a man, she then shows all her
love and desire. A man should gather from the actions of the woman of
what disposition she is, and in what way she likes to be enjoyed.
A woman during her monthly courses, a woman who has been lately
confined, and a fat woman should not be made to act the part of a man."

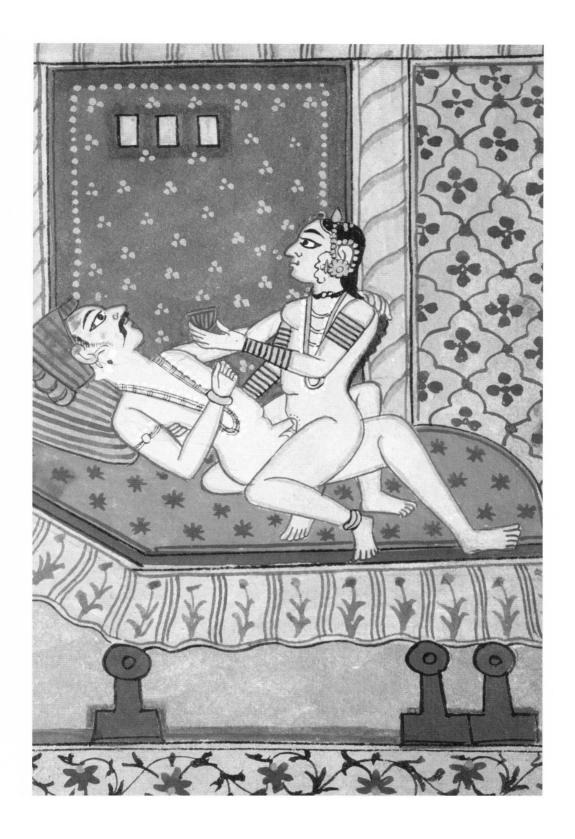

CHAPTER 9

Of the Auparishtaka[7] or mouth congress

There are two kinds of eunuchs, those that are disguised as males, and those that are disguised as females. Eunuchs disguised as females imitate their dress, speech, gestures, tenderness, timidity, simplicity, softness and bashfulness. The acts that are done on the *jaghana* or middle parts of women, are done in the mouths of these eunuchs, and this is called *Auparishtaka*. These eunuchs derive their imaginable pleasure, and their livelihood from this kind of congress, and they lead the life of courtesans. So much concerning eunuchs disguised as females.

7: This practice appears to have been prevalent in some parts of India from a very ancient time. The "*Shushruta*", a work on medicine some 2,000 years old, describes the wounding of the *lingam* with the teeth as one of the causes of a disease treated upon in that work. Traces of the practice are found as far back as the 8th century, for various kinds of the *Auparishtaka* are represented in the sculptures of many Shaiva temples at Bhuvaneshwara, near Cuttack, in Orissa, and which were built about that period. From these sculptures being found in such places, it would seem that this practice was popular in that part of the country at that time. It does not seem to be so prevalent now in Hindustan, its place perhaps is filled up by the practice of sodomy, introduced since the Mahomedan period.

Eunuchs disguised as males keep their desires secret, and when they wish to do anything they lead the life of shampooers. Under the pretence of shampooing, a eunuch of this kind embraces and draws towards himself the thighs of the man whom he is shampooing, and after this he touches the joints of his thighs and his *jaghana*, or central portions of his body. Then, if he finds the *lingam* of the man erect, he presses it with his hands, and chaffs him for getting into that state. If after this, and after knowing his intention, the man does not tell the eunuch to proceed, then the latter does it of his own accord and begins the congress. If however he is ordered by the man to do it, then he disputes with him, and only consents at last with difficulty.

The following eight things are then done by the eunuch one after
the other:

1. *The nominal congress*
When, holding the man's *lingam* with his hand, and placing it
between his lips, the eunuch moves about his mouth, it is called the
"nominal congress".

2. *Biting the sides*
When, covering the end of the *lingam* with his fingers collected together
like the bud of a plant or flower, the eunuch presses the sides of it with
his lips, using his teeth also, it is called "biting the sides".

3. *Pressing outside*
When, being desired to proceed, the eunuch presses the end of the
lingam with his lips closed together, and kisses it as if he were drawing it
out, it is called the "outside pressing".

4. *Pressing inside*

When, being asked to go on, he put the *lingam* further into his mouth, and presses it with his lips and then takes it out, it is called the "inside pressing".

5. *Kissing*

When, holding the *lingam* in his hand, the eunuch kisses it as if he were kissing the lower lip, it is called "kissing".

6. *Rubbing*

When, after kissing it, he touches it with his tongue everywhere, and passes the tongue over the end of it, it is called "rubbing".

7. *Sucking a mango fruit*

When, in the same way, he puts the half of it into his mouth, and forcibly kisses and sucks it, this is called "sucking a mango fruit".

8. *Swallowing up*

And lastly, when, with the consent of the man, the eunuch puts the whole *lingam* into his mouth, and presses it to the very end, as if he were going to swallow it up, it is called "swallowing up".

At the end of each of these the eunuch expresses his wish to stop, but when one of them is finished, the man desires him to do another, and after that is done, then the one that follows it, and so on.

Striking, scratching, and other things may also be done during this kind of congress.

The *Auparishtaka* is practised only by unchaste and wanton women, female attendants and serving maids, i.e. those who are not married to anybody, but who live by shampooing.

The Acharyas (i.e. ancient and venerable authors) are of opinion that this *Auparishtaka* is the work of a dog and not of a man, because it is a low practice, and opposed to the orders of the Holy Writ, and because the man himself suffers by bringing his *lingam* into contact with the mouths of eunuchs and women. But Vatsyayana says that the orders of the Holy Writ do not affect those who resort to courtesans, and the law prohibits the practice of the *Auparishtaka* with married women only. As regards the injury to the male, that can be easily remedied.

The people of Eastern India do not resort to women who practise the *Auparishtaka*.

The people of Ahichhatra resort to such women, but do nothing with them, so far as the mouth is concerned.

The people of Saketa do with these women every kind of mouth congress, while the people of Nagara do not practise this, but do every other thing.

The people of the Shurasena country, on the southern bank of the Jumna, do everything without any hesitation, for they say that women being naturally unclean, no one can be certain about their character, their purity, their conduct, their practices, their confidences, or their speech. They are not however on this account to be abandoned, because religious law, on the authority of which they are reckoned pure, lays down that the udder of a cow is clean at the time of milking, though the

mouth of a cow, and also the mouth of her calf, are considered unclean by the Hindoos. Again a dog is clean when he seizes a deer in hunting, though food touched by a dog is otherwise considered very unclean. A bird is clean when it causes a fruit to fall from a tree by pecking at it, though things eaten by crows and other birds are considered unclean. And the mouth of a woman is clean for kissing and such like things at the time of sexual intercourse. Vatsyayana moreover thinks that in all these things connected with love, everybody should act according to the custom of his country, and his own inclination.

There are also the following verses on the subject.

"The male servants of some men carry on the mouth congress with their masters. It is also practised by some citizens, who know each other well, among themselves. Some women of the harem, when they are amorous, do the acts of the mouth on the yonis of one another, and some men do the same thing with women. The way of doing this (i.e. of kissing the yoni) should be known from kissing the mouth. When a man and woman lie down in an inverted order, i.e. with the head of the one towards the feet of the other and carry on this congress, it is called the "congress of a crow."

For the sake of such things courtesans abandon men possessed of good qualities, liberal and clever, and become attached to low persons, such as slaves and elephant drivers. The *Auparishtaka*, or mouth congress, should never be done by a learned Brahman, by a minister that carries on the business of a state, or by a man of good reputation, because though the practice is allowed by the Shastras, there is no reason why it should be carried on, and need only be practised in particular cases. As for instance, the taste, and the strength, and the digestive qualities of the flesh of dogs are mentioned in works on medicine, but it does not therefore follow that it should be eaten by the wise. In the same way there are some men, some places and some times, with respect to which these practices can be made use of. A man should therefore pay regard to the place, to the time, and to the practice which is to be carried out, as also as to whether it is agreeable to his nature and to himself, and then he may or may not practise these things according to circumstances. But after all, these things being done secretly, and the mind of the man being fickle, how can it be known what any person will do at any particular time and for any particular purpose.

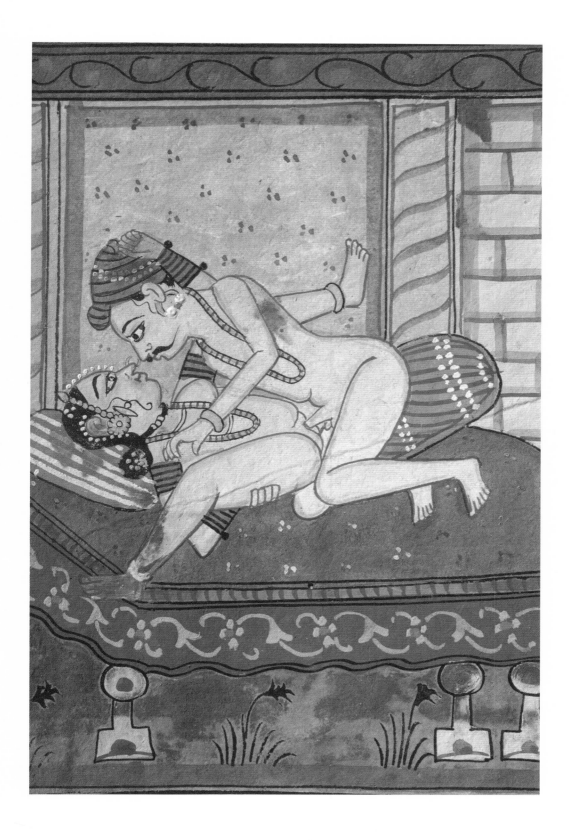

CHAPTER 10

Of the way how to begin and how to end the congress

In the pleasure-room, decorated with flowers, and fragrant with perfumes, attended by his friends and servants, the citizen should receive the woman, who will come bathed and dressed, and will invite her to take refreshment and to drink freely. He should then seat her on his left side, and holding her hair, and touching also the end and knot of her garment, he should gently embrace her with his right arm. They should then carry on an amusing conversation on various subjects, and may also talk suggestively of things which would be considered as coarse, or not to be mentioned generally in society. They may then sing, either with or without gesticulations, and play on musical instruments, talk about the arts, and persuade each other to drink. At last when the woman is overcome with love and desire, the citizen should dismiss the people that may be with him, giving them flowers, ointment, and betel leaves, and then when the two are left alone, they should proceed as has been already described in the previous chapters.

Such is the beginning of sexual union. At the end of the congress, the lovers with modesty, and not looking at each other, should go separately

to the washing-room. After this, sitting in their own places, they should eat some betel leaves, and the citizen should apply with his own hand to the body of the woman some pure sandalwood ointment, or ointment of some other kind. He should then embrace her with his left arm, and with agreeable words should cause her to drink from a cup held in his own hand, or he may give her water to drink. They can then eat sweetmeats, or anything else, according to their likings, and may drink fresh juice,[8] soup, gruel, extracts of meat, sherbet, the juice of mango fruits, the extract of the juice of the citron tree mixed with sugar, or anything that may be liked in different countries, and known to be sweet, soft, and pure. The lovers may also sit on the terrace of the palace or house, and

---

8: The fresh juice of the cocoa nut tree, the date tree, and other kinds of palm trees are drunk in India. It will not keep fresh very long, but ferments rapidly, and is then distilled into liquor.

enjoy the moonlight, and carry on an agreeable conversation. At this time, too, while the woman lies in his lap, with her face towards the moon, the citizen should show her the different planets, the morning star, the polar star, and the seven Rishis, or Great Bear.

This is the end of sexual union.

Congress is of the following kinds:

1. *Loving congress*
When a man and a woman, who have been in love with each other for some time, come together with great difficulty, or when one of the two returns from a journey, or is reconciled after having been separated on account of a quarrel, then congress is called the "loving congress". It is carried on according to the liking of the lovers, and as long as they choose.

2. *Congress of subsequent love*
When two persons come together, while their love for each other is still in its infancy, their congress is called the "congress of subsequent love".

3. *Congress of artificial love*
When a man carries on the congress by exciting himself by means of the sixty-four ways, such as kissing, etc., etc., or when a man and a woman come together, though in reality they are both attached to different persons, their congress is then called "congress of artificial love". At this time all the ways and means mentioned in the Kama Shastra should be used.

4. *Congress of transferred love*
When a man, from the beginning to the end of the congress, though having connection with the woman, thinks all the time that he is enjoying another one whom he loves, it is called the "congress of transferred love".

5. *Congress like that of eunuchs*
Congress between a man and a female water carrier, or a female servant of a caste lower than his own, lasting only until the desire is satisfied, is

called "congress like that of eunuchs". Here external touches, kisses, and manipulations are not to be employed.

6. *Deceitful congress*
The congress between a courtesan and a rustic, and that between citizens and the women of villages, and bordering countries, is called, "deceitful congress".

7. *Congress of spontaneous love*
The congress that takes place between two persons who are attached to one another, and which is done according to their own liking is called "spontaneous congress".

Thus ends the kinds of congress.

We shall now speak of love quarrels
A woman who is very much in love with a man cannot bear to hear
the name of her rival mentioned, or to have any conversation regarding
her, or to be addressed by her name through mistake. If such takes
place, a great quarrel arises, and the woman cries, becomes angry,
tosses her hair about, strikes her lover, falls from her bed or seat, and,
casting aside her garlands and ornaments, throws herself down on
the ground.

At this time, the lover should attempt to reconcile her with conciliatory words, and should take her up carefully and place her on her bed. But she, not replying to his questions, and with increased anger, should bend down his head by pulling his hair, and having kicked him once, twice, or thrice on his arms, head, bosom or back, should then proceed to the door of the room. Dattaka says that she should then sit angrily near the door and shed tears, but should not go out, because she would be found fault with for going away. After a time, when she thinks that the conciliatory words and actions of her lover have reached their utmost, she should then embrace him, talking to him with harsh and reproachful words, but at the same time showing a loving desire for congress.

When the woman is in her own house, and has quarrelled with her lover, she should go to him and show how angry she is, and leave him. Afterwards the citizen having sent the *Vita*, the *Vidushaka* or the *Pithamurda* to pacify her, she should accompany them back to the house, and spend the night with her lover.

Thus end the love quarrels.

In conclusion

A man, employing the sixty-four means mentioned by Babhravya, obtains his object, and enjoys the woman of the first quality. Though he may speak well on other subjects, if he does not know the sixty-four divisions, no great respect is paid to him in the assembly of the learned. A man, devoid of other knowledge, but well acquainted with the sixty-four divisions, becomes a leader in any society of men and women. What man will not respect the sixty-four parts,[9] considering they are respected by the learned, by the cunning, and by the courtesans. As the sixty-four parts are respected, are charming, and add to the talent of women, they are called by the Acharyas dear to women. A man skilled in the sixty-four parts is looked upon with love by his own wife, by the wives of others, and by courtesans.

9: A definition of the sixty-four parts, or divisions, is given in Chapter 2.

CHAPTER 11

On personal adornment; on subjugating the hearts of others; and on tonic medicines

When a person fails to obtain the object of his desires by any of the ways previously related, he should then have recourse to other ways of attracting others to himself.

Now, good looks, good qualities, youth, and liberality are the chief and most natural means of making a person agreeable in the eyes of others.

But in the absence of these a man or a woman must have resort to artificial means, or to art, and the following are some recipes that may be found useful.

a. An ointment made of the *tabernamontana coronaria*, the *costus speciosus* or *arabicus*, and the *flacourtia cataphracta*, can be used as an unguent of adornment.

b. If a fine powder is made of the above plants, and applied to the wick of a lamp, which is made to burn with the oil of blue vitriol, the black pigment or lamp black produced therefrom, when applied to the eyelashes, has the effect of making a person look lovely.

c. The oil of the hog weed, the *echites putescens*, the *sarina* plant, the *yellow amaranth*, and the leaf of the *nymphæ*, if applied to the body, has the same effect.

d. A black pigment from the same plants produces a similar effect.

e. By eating the powder of the *nelumbrium speciosum*, the *blue lotus*, and the *mesna roxburghii*, with *ghee* and honey, a man becomes lovely in the eyes of others.

f. The above things, together with the *tabernamontana coronaria*, and the *xanthochymus pictorius*, if used as an ointment, produce the same results.

g. If the bone of a peacock or of a hyena be covered with gold, and tied on the right hand, it makes a man lovely in the eyes of other people.

h. In the same way, if a bead, made of the seed of the *jujube*, or of the conch shell, be enchanted by the incantations mentioned in the *Atharvana Veda*, or by the incantations of those well skilled in the science of magic, and tied on the hand, it produces the same result as described above.

i. When a female attendant arrives at the age of puberty, her master should keep her secluded, and when men ardently desire her on account of her seclusion, and on account of the difficulty of approaching her, he should then bestow her hand on such a person as may endow her with wealth and happiness.

This is a means of increasing the loveliness of a person in the eyes of others.

In the same way, when the daughter of a courtesan arrives at the age of puberty, the mother should get together a lot of young men of the same age, disposition, and knowledge as her daughter, and tell them that she would give her in marriage to the person who would give her presents of a particular kind.

After this the daughter should be kept in seclusion as far as possible, and the mother should give her in marriage to the man who may be ready to give her the presents agreed upon. If the mother is unable to get so much out of the man, she should show some of her own things as having been given to the daughter by the bridegroom.

Or, the mother may allow her daughter to be married to the man privately, as if she was ignorant of the whole affair, and then pretending that it has come to her knowledge, she may give her consent to the union.

The daughter, too, should make herself attractive to the sons of wealthy citizens, unknown to her mother, and make them attached to her, and for this purpose should meet them at the time of learning to sing, and in places where music is played, and at the houses of other people, and then request her mother, through a female friend, or

servant, to be allowed to unite herself to the man who is most agreeable to her.[10]

When the daughter of a courtesan is thus given to a man, the ties of marriage should be observed for one year, and after that she may do what she likes. But even after the end of the year, when otherwise engaged, if she should be now and then invited by her first husband to come and see him, she should put aside her present gain, and go to him for the night.

Such is the mode of temporary marriage among courtesans, and of increasing their loveliness, and their value in the eyes of others. What has been said about them should also be understood to apply to the daughters of dancing women, whose mothers should give them only to

---

10: It is a custom of the courtesans of Oriental countries to give their daughters temporarily in marriage when they come of age, and after they have received an education in the Kama Sutra and other arts.

such persons as are likely to become useful to them in various ways.

Thus end the ways of making oneself lovely in the eyes of others.

a. If a man, after anointing his *lingam* with a mixture of the powders of the white thorn apple, the long pepper, and the black pepper and honey, engages in sexual union with a woman, he makes her subject to his will.

b. The application of a mixture of the leaf of the plant *vatodbhranta*, of the flowers thrown on a human corpse when carried out to be burnt, and the powder of the bones of the peacock, and of the *jiwanjiva* bird, produces the same effect.

c. The remains of a kite who has died a natural death, ground into powder, and mixed with cowach and honey, has also the same effect.

d. Anointing oneself with an ointment made of the plant *emblica myrabolans* has the power of subjecting women to one's will.

e. If a man cuts into small pieces the sprouts of the *vajnasunhi* plant, and dips them into a mixture of red arsenic and sulphur, and then dries them seven times, and applies this powder mixed with honey to his *lingam*, he can subjugate a woman to his will directly that he has had sexual union with her, or, if, by burning these very sprouts at night and looking at the smoke, he sees a golden moon behind, he will then be successful with any woman; or if he throws some of the powder of these same sprouts mixed with the excrement of a monkey upon a maiden, she will not be given in marriage to anybody else.

f. If pieces of the arris root are dressed with the oil of the mango, and placed for six months in a hole made in the trunk of the sisu tree, and are then taken out and made up into an ointment, and applied to the *lingam*, this is said to serve as the means of subjugating women.

g. If the bone of a camel is dipped into the juice of the plant *eclipta prostata*, and then burnt, and the black pigment produced from its ashes is placed in a box also made of the bone of a camel, and applied together

with antimony to the eyelashes with a pencil also made of the bone of a camel, then that pigment is said to be very pure, and wholesome for the eyes, and serves as a means of subjugating others to the person who uses it. The same effect can be produced by black pigment made of the bones of hawks, vultures, and peacocks.

Thus end the ways of subjugating others to one's own will.

Now the means of increasing sexual vigour are as follows:

a. A man obtains sexual vigour by drinking milk mixed with sugar, the root of the *uchchata* plant, the *piper chaba*, and liquorice.

b. Drinking milk mixed with sugar, and having the testicle of a ram or a goat boiled in it, is also productive of vigour.

c. The drinking of the juice of the *hedysarum gangeticum*, the *kuili*, and the *kshirika* plant mixed with milk, produces the same effect.

d. The seed of the long pepper along with the seeds of the *sanseviera roxburghiana*, and the *hedysarum gangeticum* plant, all pounded together, and mixed with milk, is productive of a similar result.

e. According to ancient authors, if a man pounds the seeds or roots of the *trapa bispinosa*, the *kasurika*, the *tuscan* jasmine, and liquorice, together with the *kshirakapoli* (a kind of onion), and puts the powder into milk mixed with sugar and *ghee*, and having boiled the whole mixture on a moderate fire, drinks the paste so formed, he will be able to enjoy innumerable women.

f. In the same way, if a man mixes rice with the eggs of the sparrow, and having boiled this in milk, adds to it *ghee* and honey, and drinks as much of it as necessary, this will produce the same effect.

g. If a man takes the outer covering of sesamum seeds, and soaks them with the eggs of sparrows, and then, having boiled them in milk, mixed with sugar and *ghee*, along with the fruits of the *trapa bispinosa* and the *kasurika* plant, and adding to it the flour of wheat and beans, and then drinks this composition, he is said to be able to enjoy many women.

h. If *ghee*, honey, sugar, and liquorice in equal quantities, the juice of the fennel plant, and milk are mixed together, this nectar-like composition is said to be holy, and provocative of sexual vigour, a preservative of life, and sweet to the taste.

i. The drinking of a paste composed of the *asparagus racemosus*, the *shvadaushtra* plant, the *guduchi* plant, the long pepper, and liquorice, boiled in milk, honey, and *ghee*, in the spring, is said to have the same effect as the above.

j. Boiling the *asparagus racemosus*, and the *shvadaushtra* plant, along with the pounded fruits of the *premna spinosa* in water, and drinking the same, is said to act in the same way.

k. Drinking boiled *ghee*, or clarified butter, in the morning during the spring season, is said to be beneficial to health and strength, and agreeable to the taste.

l. If the powder of the seed of the *shvadaushtra* plant and the flower of barley are mixed together in equal parts, and a portion of it, i.e. two *palas* in weight, is eaten every morning on getting up, it has the same effect as the preceding recipe.

There are also verses on the subject as follows:

"The means[11] *of producing love and sexual vigour should be
learnt from the science of medicine, from the Vedas, from those who are
learned in the arts of magic, and from confidential relatives.
No means should be tried which are doubtful in their effects, which are
likely to cause injury to the body, which involve the death of animals,
and which bring us in contact with impure things.
Such means should only be used as are holy, acknowledged to be good,
and approved of by Brahmans, and friends."*

11: From the earliest times Oriental authors have occupied themselves about aphrodisiacs. The following note on the subject is taken from page 29 of a translation of the *Hindoo Art of Love*, otherwise the *Anunga Runga*: "Most Eastern treatises divide aphrodisiacs into two different kinds: 1., the mechanical or natural, such as scarification, flagellation, etc.; and 2., the medicinal or artificial. To the former belong the application of insects, as is practised by some savage races; and all orientalists will remember the tale of the old Brahman, whose young wife insisted upon his being again stung by a wasp."

CHAPTER 12

Of the ways of exciting desire, and miscellaneous experiments, and recipes

If a man is unable to satisfy a *Hastini*, or elephant woman, he should have recourse to various means to excite her passion. At the commencement he should rub her *yoni* with his hand or fingers, and not begin to have intercourse with her until she becomes excited, or experiences pleasure. This is one way of exciting a woman.

Or, he may make use of certain *Apadravyas*, or things which are put on or around the *lingam* to supplement its length or its thickness, so as to fit it to the *yoni*. In the opinion of Babhravya, these *Apadravyas* should be made of gold, silver, copper, iron, ivory, buffalo's horn, various kinds of wood, tin or lead, and should be soft, cool, provocative of sexual vigour, and well fitted to serve the intended purpose. Vatsyayana, however, says that they may be made according to the natural liking of each individual.

The following are the different kinds of *Apadravyas*.

1. "The armlet" (*Valaya*) should be of the same size as the *lingam*, and

should have its outer surface made rough with globules.

2. "The couple" (*Sanghati*) is formed of two armlets.

3. "The bracelet" (*Chudaka*) is made by joining three or more armlets, until they come up to the required length of the *lingam*.

4. "The single bracelet" is formed by wrapping a single wire around the *lingam*, according to its dimensions.

5. The *Kantuka* or *Jalaka* is a tube open at both ends, with a hole through it, outwardly rough and studded with soft globules, and made to fit the side of the *yoni*, and tied to the waist.

When such a thing cannot be obtained, then a tube made of the wood apple, or tubular stalk of the bottle gourd, or a reed made soft with oil and extracts of plants, and tied to the waist with strings, may be made use of, as also a row of soft pieces of wood tied together.

The above are the things that can be used in connection with or in the place of the *lingam*.

The people of the southern countries think that true sexual pleasure cannot be obtained without perforating the *lingam*, and they therefore cause it to be pierced like the lobes of the ears of an infant pierced for earrings.

Now, when a young man perforates his *lingam* he should pierce it with a harp instrument, and then stand in water so long as the blood continues to flow. At night he should engage in sexual intercourse, even with vigour, so as to clean the hole. After this he should continue to wash the hole with decoctions, and increase the size by putting into it small pieces of cane, and the *wrightia antidysenterica*, and thus gradually enlarging the orifice. It may also be washed with liquorice mixed with honey, and the size of the hole increased by the fruit stalks of the *sima-patra* plant. The hole should be anointed with a small quantity of oil.

In the hole made in the *lingam* a man may put *Apadravyas* of various forms, such as the "round", the "round on one side", the "wooden mortar", the "flower", the "armlet", the "bone of the heron", the "goad of the elephant", the "collection of eight balls", the "lock of hair", the

"place where four roads meet", and other things named according to their forms and means of using them. All these *Apadravyas* should be rough on the outside according to their requirements.

The ways of enlarging the *lingam* must be now related.

When a man wishes to enlarge his *lingam*, he should rub it with the bristles of certain insects that live in trees, and then, after rubbing it for ten nights with oils, he should again rub it with the bristles as before. By continuing to do this a swelling will be gradually produced in the *lingam*, and he should then lie on a cot, and cause his *lingam* to hang down through a hole in the cot. After this he should take away all the pain from the swelling by using cool concoctions. The swelling, which is called "*Suka*", and is often brought about among the people of the Dravida country, lasts for life.

If the *lingam* is rubbed with the following things, *viz.* the plant *physalis flexuosa*, the *shavara-kandaka* plant, the *jalasuka* plant, the fruit of the egg plant, the butter of a she-buffalo, the *hastri-charma* plant, and the juice of the *vajra-rasa* plant, a swelling lasting for one month will be produced.

By rubbing it with oil boiled in the concoctions of the above things, the same effect will be produced, but lasting for six months.

The enlargement of the *lingam* is also effected by rubbing it or moistening it with oil boiled on a moderate fire along with the seeds of the pomegranate, and the cucumber, the juices of the *valuka* plant, the *hasti-charma* plant, and the egg-plant.

In addition to the above, other means may be learnt from experienced and confidential persons.

The miscellaneous experiments and recipes are as follows:

a. If a man mixes the powder of the milk hedge plant, and the *kantaka* plant with the excrement of a monkey, and the powdered root of the *lanjalalika* plant, and throws this mixture on a woman, she will not love anybody else afterwards.

b. If a man thickens the juice of the fruits of the *cassia fistula*, and the *eugenia jambolana* by mixing them with the powder of the *soma* plant, the *vernonia anthelmintica*, the *eclipta prostata*, and the *lohopa-jihirka*, and applies this composition to the *yoni* of a woman, and then has sexual intercourse with her, his love for her will be destroyed.

c. The same effect is produced if a man has connection with a woman who has bathed in the butter-milk of a she-buffalo mixed with the powders of the *gopalika* plant, the *banu-padika* plant, and the yellow amaranth.

d. An ointment made of the flowers of the *nauclea cadamba*, the hog plum, and the *eugenia jambolana*, and used by a woman, causes her to be disliked by her husband.

e. Garlands made of the above flowers, when worn by the woman, produce the same effect.

f. An ointment made of the fruit of the *asteracantha longifolia* (*kokilaksha*) will contract the *yoni* of a *Hastini* or elephant woman, and this contraction lasts for one night.

g. An ointment made by pounding the roots of the *nelumbrium speciosum*, and of the blue lotus, and the powder of the plant *physalis flexuosa* mixed with *ghee* and honey, will enlarge the *yoni* of the *Mrigi* or deer woman.

h. An ointment made of the fruit of the *emblica myrabolans* soaked in

the milky juice of the milk hedge plant, of the *soma* plant, the *calotropis gigantea*, and the juice of the fruit of the *vernonia anthelmintica*, will make the hair white.

i. The juice of the roots of the *madayantaka* plant, the yellow amaranth, the *anjanika* plant, the *clitoria ternateea*, and the *shlakshnaparni* plant, used as a lotion, will make the hair grow.

j. An ointment made by boiling the above roots in oil, and rubbed in, will make the hair black, and will also gradually restore hair that has fallen off.

k. If lac is saturated seven times in the sweat of the testicle of a white horse, and applied to a red lip, the lip will become white.

l. The colour of the lips can be regained by means of the *madayantika* and other plants mentioned above under (i).

m. A woman who hears a man playing on a reed pipe which has been dressed with the juices of the *bahupadika* plant, the *tabernamontana coronaria*, the *costus speciosus* or *arabicus*, the *pinus deodora*, the *euphorbia antiquorum*, the *vajra* and the *kantaka* plant, becomes his slave.

n. If food be mixed with the fruit of the thorn apple (*Dathura*) it causes intoxication.

o. If water be mixed with oil and the ashes of any kind of grass except the *kusha* grass, it becomes the colour of milk.

p. If yellow *myrabolans*, the hog plum, the *shrawana* plant, and the *priyangu* plant be all pounded together, and applied to iron pots, these pots become red.

q. If a lamp, trimmed with oil extracted from the *shrawana* and *priyangn* plants, its wick being made of cloth and the slough of the skins of snakes, is lighted, and long pieces of wood placed near it, those pieces of wood will resemble so many snakes.

r. Drinking the milk of a white cow who has a white calf at her feet is auspicious, produces fame, and preserves life.

s. The blessings of venerable Brahmans, well propitiated, have the same effect.

There are also some verses in conclusion:

> "Thus have I written in a few words the 'Science of love',
> after reading the texts of ancient authors, and following the ways
> of enjoyment mentioned in them."

> "He who is acquainted with the true principles of this science pays
> regard to Dharma, Artha, Kama, and to his own experiences, as well as to

the teachings of others, and does not act simply on the dictates of his own desire. As for the errors in the science of love which I have mentioned in this work, on my own authority as an author, I have, immediately after mentioning them, carefully censured and prohibited them."

"An act is never looked upon with indulgence for the simple reason that it is authorised by the science, because it ought to be remembered that it is the intention of the science, that the rules which it contains should only be acted upon in particular cases. After reading and considering the works of Babhravya and other ancient authors, and thinking over the meaning of the rules given by them, the Kama Sutra was composed, according to the precepts of Holy Writ, for the benefit of the world, by Vatsyayana, while leading the life of a religious student, and wholly engaged in the contemplation of the Deity."

"This work is not intended to be used merely as an instrument for satisfying our desires. A person, acquainted with the true principles of this science, and who preserves his Dharma, Artha, and Kama, and has regard for the practices of the people, is sure to obtain the mastery over his senses."

"In short, an intelligent and prudent person, attending to Dharma and Artha, and attending to Kama also, without becoming the slave of his passions, obtains success in everything that he may undertake."

Glossary

Apadravyas Things which are put on or around the *lingam* to supplement its length or its thickness

Auparishtaka Mouth congress

Hastini Elephant woman

Jaghana Middle parts of women

Jataveshtitaka Embrace – when a woman clings to a man as a "twining of a creeper"

Kshiraniraka When lovers embrace each other while the woman is sitting on the lap of the man or in front of him, or on a bed, then it is called an embrace like a "mixture of milk and water"

Lingam Penis

Mrigi Deer woman

Tila-Tandulaka Embrace – when lovers lie on a bed, with arms and thighs encircled and rubbing up against them, this is called an embrace like "the mixture of sesamum seed with rice"

Vadawa Mare woman

Vrikshadhirudhaka Embrace – when a woman places one of her feet on the foot of her lover, and the other on one of his thighs, like "climbing of a tree"

Yoni Vagina

Index